EDGE BOOKS

The Kids' Guide to

MUMMIES

BY JOAN AXELROD-CONTRADA

Consultant:

Leo Depuydt, Professor
Department of Egyptology and Ancient Western Asian Studies
Brown University
Providence, Rhode Island

CAPSTONE PRESS
a capstone imprint

Edge Books are published by Capstone Press,
151 Good Counsel Drive, P.O. Box 669, Mankato, Minnesota 56002.
www.capstonepub.com

Library of Congress Cataloging-in-Publication Data
Axelrod-Contrada, Joan.
  The kids' guide to mummies / by Joan Axelrod-Contrada.
    p. cm. — (Edge books. Kids' guides)
  Includes bibliographical references and index.
  Summary: "Describes mummies throughout history, from ancient Egypt to
modern times"—Provided by publisher.
  ISBN 978-1-4296-5441-8 (hardcover)
  1. Mummies—Juvenile literature. I. Title.
  GN293.A94 2011
  393'.3—dc22   2010035017

Editorial Credits
Angie Kaelberer, editor; Kyle Grenz, designer; Eric Gohl, media researcher;
    Michelle Biedscheid, production specialist

Photo Credits
Alamy/Ancient Art & Architecture Collection Ltd, 9 (bottom); The Art Archive,
    15, 18, 19; Christine Osborne Pictures, 7 (bottom); Eye Ubiquitous, 20;
    Images of Africa Photobank, 17 (bottom); John T. Fowler, 25; Mary Evans
    Picture Library, 9 (top), 14; The Print Collector, 12 (bottom); Robert
    Harding Picture Library Ltd, 21, 24
AP Images, 26
BigStockPhoto.com/Quintanilla, 12 (top)
Corbis/Sygma/Vienna Report Agency, 22
Getty Images Inc./AFP, 29; Jeff Topping, 28; Marc Deville, 13; National
    Geographic/Kenneth Garrett, 17 (top); Patrick Landmann, 10
Library of Congress, 16
Newscom/AFP/Getty Images, 6, 23
Shutterstock/Alfio Ferlito, 11; Carlos E. Santa Maria, cover (left); Jose Ignacio
    Soto, 7 (top); LacoKozyna, cover (top); Laurin Rinder, 27; Rachelle
    Burnside, cover (right); Studio 37, 4; velefante, 5

Printed in the United States of America in Stevens Point, Wisconsin.
092010   005934WZS11

TABLE OF CONTENTS

ALL ABOUT MUMMIES

Mummies. Just hearing the word can send a chill down your spine. You picture the walking dead wrapped in bandages, ready to chase after you. That is how mummies appear in horror movies.

But are these stories even close to being true? Well, no. But mummies do exist and have for thousands of years.

Fun Fact:

The word "mummy" comes from the Persian word "mummia," which was a black, tarlike substance now called bitumen. Bitumen may have been used in making mummies at one time.

4

REAL MUMMIES

Real-life mummies have never risen from the dead to hurt the living. Instead, they're simply dead bodies that have been preserved. Their skin stays on the body, so they don't turn into bony skeletons.

For thousands of years, humans have learned secrets of preserving the dead. In about 3000 BC, ancient Egyptians began wrapping bodies in cloth coated with **resin** to preserve them. Other cultures **embalmed** their dead and are still doing so today.

GINGER

Not all mummies are made by people. Bodies sometimes become mummies naturally, especially in very dry or cold climates. Scientists nicknamed one famous natural mummy "Ginger" because of his red hair. Ginger was buried in a shallow grave more than 5,000 years ago near Gebelein, Egypt. The hot desert sands sucked up the moisture from his body. It was then protected from flesh-eating bacteria that need water to grow.

resin—a sticky substance that comes from the sap of some trees

embalm—to preserve a dead body so that it does not decay

No place is more famous for its mummies than ancient Egypt. Egyptians learned about the natural process of mummy making by watching bodies dry in the hot desert. They perfected the process and turned it into an art form.

Ancient Egyptians believed people who had led good lives on Earth went to a perfect afterlife called Yaru. The body needed to be preserved to provide shelter for the soul after death.

Embalmers offered several levels of mummification. Only the wealthy could afford the most elaborate forms.

OSIRIS LEGEND

A myth about the god-king Osiris inspired the Egyptians to mummify their dead. The legend says that wise King Osiris brought agriculture and civilization to his people. But his younger brother, Seth, was jealous of Osiris' success.

One day Seth drowned Osiris and scattered his body parts throughout Egypt. Osiris' wife, Isis, searched until she found the parts. Then she asked the god Anubis to help preserve the body. Using magic, she brought Osiris back to life. He went on to become god of the underworld. Souls had to pass through this dark, dangerous area on their way to Yaru.

Fun Fact:

Egyptians believed the gods weighed the hearts of dead people. If the heart was heavy with sin, the monster Ammut ate it. The person's soul was then not allowed into the afterlife.

MAKING AN EGYPTIAN MUMMY

Through trial and error, Egyptians figured out how to keep dead bodies fresh, right down to their eyelashes. Mummification involved a number of workers and steps.

STEP 1: CLEANING OUT THE BODY

First the body was purified. A chief priest watched as the embalmers washed the body. Then a worker sliced open the body and removed the lungs, stomach, intestine, and liver. But the heart stayed in place. Egyptians believed the heart was the center of human intelligence. They didn't think the brain was important at all. They used a wire hook to remove the brain through the nose and then threw it away.

After the organs were removed, workers put each one in a canopic jar. They then filled the mummy's chest cavity with spices and wine. These materials covered up the rotting smell of the dead body.

During embalming, the chief priest wore a mask of Anubis, the jackal-headed god of embalming.

The lid of each jar showed a different god. Hapy had an ape's head. He guarded the lungs. Duamutef, who had the head of a wild dog, held the stomach. The hawk-headed god Qebhsenuef protected the intestines. Imsety, who had a human head, held the liver.

CANOPIC JARS

jackal—a type of wild dog that feeds on dead animals

STEP 2: DRYING THE BODY

Embalmers laid bodies on drying beds covered with a natural mineral called natron. The drying process took about 40 days.

STEP 3: DECORATING THE BODY

Once the body was dry, workers brought it to another area called the *per nefer*, which means "beautiful house." First they stuffed the body with materials such as sawdust, dry plants, or resin. After waterproofing the mummy with resin, they added makeup. Some mummies also had their fingernails covered with gold.

Egyptians painted a mummy's face and sometimes its body with colored clay called ocher. They used red ocher for men and yellow for women. These colors were based on people's real-life complexions. Men were tanned from working outdoors, while women were paler.

Often embalmers put a scarab amulet, or charm, over the heart. The scarab is a dung beetle that was **sacred** to Egyptians. Its life cycle reminded them of that of the Sun.

According to an Egyptian legend, the world began when a mound of earth rose up from the waters. The mound contained the Sun. The scarab laid its eggs in a mound of dung, which it rolled across the ground to its burrow. Egyptians believed the god Khepera pushed the Sun along the sky in much the same way.

SCARAB AMULET

Fun Fact:

Ancient Egyptians placed amulets between a mummy's layers of bandages. They believed these good-luck charms protected the soul from the monsters of the underworld.

sacred— holy or having to do with religion

STEP 4: WRAPPING THE MUMMY

Egyptians wrapped their mummies in layers of linen strips. Each limb was wrapped individually.

A mask placed over the head and shoulders was the final touch. The wealthier the person, the finer the mask. Embalmers used a hardened fabric similar to papier-mâché for the masks of most mummies. Pharaohs wore masks of solid gold. In later years, portraits of the dead person painted on wood with colored wax replaced the masks.

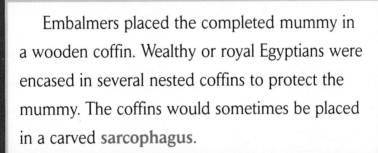

SARCOPHAGUS

Embalmers placed the completed mummy in a wooden coffin. Wealthy or royal Egyptians were encased in several nested coffins to protect the mummy. The coffins would sometimes be placed in a carved **sarcophagus**.

Women weren't the only ones who wore eye makeup and lipstick in ancient Egypt. Men did as well.

sarcophagus—a stone coffin

SECRETS OF THE TOMBS

Egyptians weren't buried in small graves as people are today. Egyptians filled their large underground tombs with food, clothes, furniture, and other things they needed for the long afterlife. Tombs of the wealthy sometimes even held chariots.

Many pharaohs were buried inside magnificent pyramids. At one time, wives and servants of the king were killed soon after he died. The ancient Egyptians believed the pharaoh needed his wives and servants to take care of him in the afterlife. About 3100 BC the Egyptians replaced human sacrifice with figurines and paintings. They believed these objects magically sprang to life to care for the dead person.

SERVANT FIGURINE

THE TOMB OF SENEFER

PROTECTING THE TOMBS

The pyramids held glittering gold and jewels. These royal resting places attracted generations of robbers.

Many tombs were designed to keep robbers away from the treasures. Some tombs had curses written on the walls that warned trespassers of horrible deaths. Other tombs included deadly traps. A boulder might crash down from over a doorway. Or a trap door in the floor opened into a deep, dark pit.

KING TUT

On November 4, 1922, British archaeologist Howard Carter literally struck gold. That day, he found the tomb of King Tutankhamun, known as King Tut. The king was wearing gold sandals and a mask of solid gold. It was the first discovery of a royal tomb with almost all of its treasure undisturbed.

KING TUT'S CURSE

Several people who came in contact with Tut's mummy died soon afterward. They included Carter's sponsor Lord Carnarvon, wealthy businessman George Jay Gould, and scientists Hugh Evelyn-White and Archibald Douglas Reed. Newspaper articles claimed the deaths were caused by a curse on anyone who disturbed Tut's body.

No such curse existed. Lord Carnarvon died of an infected mosquito bite, while Gould and Reed died of illnesses. Evelyn-White committed suicide. And Howard Carter, who disturbed the tomb in the first place, lived another 17 years before dying of cancer. But the curse myth made a good story.

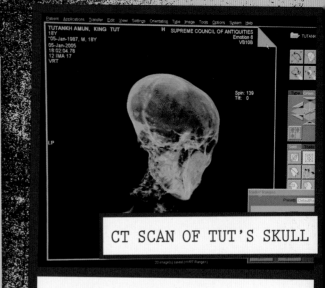

CT SCAN OF TUT'S SKULL

Fun Fact:

King Tut's face was so well preserved that his jaw showed his slightly buck teeth.

WAS KING TUT MURDERED?

King Tut ruled over Egypt as a boy and a teenager. His death at the age of 19 has long puzzled historians. Many have turned to his mummy for answers.

When scientists found a hole in King Tut's skull, some believed that he had been murdered. But a CT scan in 2006 proved this wasn't true. The hole in the skull had been made after Tut's death. Researchers now believe Tut died from malaria and a broken leg that became infected.

archaeologist—a scientist who studies how people lived in the past

malaria—a serious disease that people can get from mosquito bites

ANIMAL MUMMIES

Ancient Egyptians mummified all sorts of animals—everything from tiny insects to massive bulls. Animals represented the spirits of the gods. People treated their pet dogs, cats, and even monkeys with great respect and affection.

PET MUMMIES

Cats earned a special place in people's hearts because they caught pesky mice and rats. Several cities had cemeteries just for cats. People buried their mummified felines with live mice and rats to eat in the next world.

Many Egyptians worshiped the cat goddess, Bastet. She had the head of a cat and the body of a woman. Bastet's temple was located in the city of Bubastis. At the temple, priests cared for many sacred cats.

Cat owners showed their grief over the deaths of their pets by shaving their eyebrows.

THE SACRED BULL

To Egyptians, bulls were the most sacred animals of all. Many people worshiped the Apis bull. This black bull with distinctive white markings was believed to hold the spirit of the god Osiris. When the Apis bull died, it was mummified and given a funeral almost as grand as a pharaoh's. People then began searching for the next sacred bull.

Everyone knows about Egyptian mummies. But other cultures also preserved their dead. The Egyptians weren't even the first to do it.

CHILEAN MUMMIES

Thousands of years before the pharaohs, the Chinchorros of northern Chile made mummies. Beginning in about 5000 BC, they rebuilt their dead. They first removed the skin and internal organs. Next they dried the bones and attached them to twigs for reinforcement. Over this framework, they reattached the skin. They then applied a thick layer of ash paste over the body. Next they coated the body with red ocher or a metal called manganese. A clay mask covered the face, and some wore wigs of human hair. The Chinchorros may have honored the mummies by displaying them at feasts and festivals.

MUMMY BUNDLES OF PERU

About 500 years ago, Inca people in Peru mummified their dead in a sitting position. They wrapped them in layers of cloth to create bundles. Each layer contained items that the dead person might need in the afterlife, such as weapons and plates. Some of these "mummy bundles" weigh more than 200 pounds (91 kilograms).

MYSTERY MUMMIES OF CHINA

Beginning in the late 1970s, natural mummies with light brown, red, and blond hair were found in the Tarim Basin of western China. Scientists were surprised that these desert mummies looked European instead of Asian.

Researchers studied the clothes of the mummies for answers. Cherchen Man is a 6-foot, 6-inch (198-centimeter) mummy who died around 1000 BC. He wore woolen leggings in a plaid pattern similar to those worn by men in Scotland. From this clue, some historians believe that he was a Celt. These people lived in Europe from around 800 BC until AD 400. Most settled in the British Isles. But they may have come from central Asia sometime after 3000 BC and split into two groups. One group may have headed west toward Europe and the other east toward China.

Ice Mummies

Snow, ice, and cold temperatures can keep bodies frozen in time. Like the heat of the desert, extreme cold kills bacteria. Without bacteria to eat flesh, a dead body can become a natural mummy.

OTZI, THE ICEMAN

In 1991 mountain climbers found a frozen mummy in the Otzal Alps in Italy. He was nicknamed "Otzi" for the mountains where he was found. Researchers believe Otzi died about 5,300 years ago from an arrow wound in his shoulder.

Otzi has 57 tattoos. Researchers think he made them by using a needle to inject fireplace soot under his skin. The tattoos may have served as pain relief rather than decoration. Today some people relieve pain with acupuncture. This treatment involves sticking needles into pressure points in the skin.

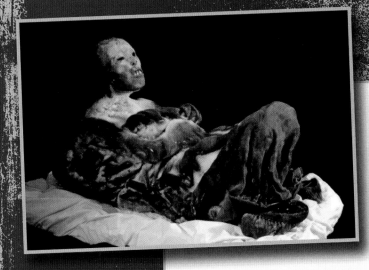

JUANITA, THE ICE MAIDEN

In 1995 scientist Johan Reinhard was exploring the Andes Mountains in Peru. He discovered the mummy of an Inca girl preserved in ice. Reinhard named the mummy Juanita, but most people know her as the Ice Maiden. Scientists believe she died about 500 years ago from a blow to the back of her head.

The Ice Maiden was probably sacrificed to the gods. The Inca believed that human sacrifice pleased the gods. The gods would then protect the rest of the community from harm.

Fun Fact:

Food companies use a process similar to ice mummification to produce lightweight items with long shelf lives. Freeze-dried foods include instant coffee and meal pouches for campers and soldiers.

Bog Mummies

Heat and cold aren't the only things that create natural mummies. Many mummies have been found in the swampy peat bogs of northern Europe. The cold, acidic bog water preserves flesh, turning it to a leathery texture. These mummies are known as bog people.

CRIMINALS OR SACRIFICES?

The bog people were Germans and Celts that lived about 2,000 years ago. Many of the bog mummies appear to have been killed violently. Some had smashed skulls or cut throats. Others had nooses around their necks or were tied to heavy rocks.

Scientists believe that people accused of some crimes were killed and dumped in the bogs. Others may have been sacrificed to the gods.

Fun Fact:

Tollund Man is probably the most famous bog mummy. He was found in Tollund, Denmark, in 1950. The well-preserved mummy still has the stubble on his chin!

peat—partly decayed plant matter found in bogs and swamps

Modern-Day Mummies

Much has changed since the days when the ancient Egyptians wrapped their dead in long strips of cloth. Today funeral directors use modern chemicals and new technology to preserve human bodies.

Yet some things do remain the same. Bodies still can be naturally preserved in deserts, ice, and bogs. In 1960 eight mummified bodies were found in the Libyan Desert. The men were crew members of the U.S. Army plane *Lady Be Good*. The plane had crashed in 1943.

LADY BE GOOD WRECKAGE

MODERN-DAY EMBALMING

Ancient Egyptians wanted to preserve bodies forever. But today's embalmers generally try to keep bodies fresh for wakes and funerals. They use an electric pump to inject embalming fluid into the circulatory system. This flushes the blood out of the body.

The Summum organization of Utah offers a modern form of mummification for people and pets. The body is preserved in a liquid bath before being wrapped in cotton gauze. The gauze is then coated with polyurethane, fiberglass, and resin. The mummy is placed in an Egyptian-style casket called a mummiform. The casket is filled with amber resin.

CRYONICS

Believers in a process called **cryonics** hope the dead can someday be brought back to life. Cryonics involves freezing bodies in liquid nitrogen. Someday advances in science may allow the bodies to be thawed and repaired. But many scientists doubt this can ever happen.

CRYONICS LAB

PLASTINATION

Anyone who has seen a traveling art exhibit called Body Worlds got a firsthand look at the process of plastination. In this process, water and fat in the body are replaced with plastic substances. Plastination allows the body to stay more flexible than other preservation methods do.

FACT VS. FICTION

Scientists study mummies to learn the secrets of how ancient people lived and died. But mummies don't have to be taken seriously all the time. Throughout the ages, people have imagined them springing back to life just for fun. Like vampires, ghosts, and werewolves, mummies turn up whenever you need a good scare.

MUMMIFIED LEADER

Perhaps the most famous modern-day mummy is that of Russian leader Vladimir Lenin. When Lenin died in 1924, his body was mummified and placed on display in a glass case in Moscow. Every 18 months, his body is removed from the case and soaked in a preservative bath. The head and hands are bathed with embalming fluid twice a week to remove any decaying spots.

cryonics—the practice of freezing a dead body in the hope of later bringing it back to life

GLOSSARY

archaeologist (ar-kee-OL-uh-jist)—a scientist who studies how people lived in the past

cryonics (kri-AH-niks)—the practice of freezing a dead body in the hope of later bringing it back to life

embalm (im-BALM)—to preserve a dead body so that it does not decay

jackal (JAK-uhl)—a type of wild dog that feeds on dead animals

malaria (muh-LAIR-ee-uh)—a serious disease that people can get from mosquito bites

peat (PEET)—partly decayed plant matter found in bogs and swamps

resin (REZ-in)—a sticky substance that comes from the sap of some trees

sacred (SAY-krid)—holy or having to do with religion

sarcophagus (sar-KAH-fuh-guhs)—a stone coffin

Read More

Biskup, Agnieszka. *Uncovering Mummies: An Isabel Soto Archaeology Adventure.* Graphic Expeditions. Mankato, Minn.: Capstone Press, 2010.

Carney, Elizabeth. *Mummies.* Science Readers. Washington, D.C.: National Geographic, 2009.

Montgomery, Heather L. *Mummies: Truth and Rumors.* Truth and Rumors. Mankato, Minn.: Capstone Press, 2010.

Internet Sites

FactHound offers a safe, fun way to find Internet sites related to this book. All of the sites on FactHound have been researched by our staff.

Here's all you do:

Visit *www.facthound.com*

Type in this code: 9781429654418

INDEX